The Little Book Of
MUSICAL TERMS

Your essential A – Z guide

Wise Publications
London/New York/Sydney/Paris/Copenhagen/Madrid

Exclusive distributors:
Music Sales Limited
8/9 Frith Street, London W1V 5TZ, England.
Music Sales Pty Limited
120 Rothschild Avenue
Rosebery, NSW 2018, Australia.

Order No.AM954866
ISBN 0-7119-7825-5
This book © Copyright 1999 by Wise Publications

Book engraved and designed by Digital Music Art

Cover design by Trickett & Webb

Printed in Great Britain by
Printwise (Haverhill) Limited, Suffolk.

Your Guarantee of Quality
As publishers, we strive to produce every book to the highest commercial
standards. Particular care has been given to specifying acid-free, neutral-sized paper
made from pulps which have not been elemental chlorine bleached. This pulp is from
farmed sustainable forests and was produced with special regard for the environment.
Throughout, the printing and binding have been planned to ensure a sturdy,
attractive publication which should give years of enjoyment.
If your copy fails to meet our high standards, please inform us and we will gladly replace it.

Music Sales' complete catalogue describes thousands of titles and is
available in full colour sections by subject, direct from Music Sales Limited.
Please state your areas of interest and send a cheque/postal order for £1.50 for postage to:
Music Sales Limited, Newmarket Road, Bury St. Edmunds, Suffolk IP33 3YB.

www.musicsales.co.uk

A capella
(I) Lit. 'in a church manner'. Music sung by unaccompanied voices.

A tempo
(I) Return to the original speed.

Accelerando
(I) Gradually increase the tempo.

Accent
A small arrow-like mark placed on a note or **chord** giving it more emphasis.

Acciaccatura
(I) Lit. 'crushed'. A note that theoretically has no duration, added before another as a decoration.

Accidental
A **sharp** (♯), **flat** (♭) or **natural** (♮) sign which raises or lowers a note by a **semitone**, or restores it to its usual pitch respectively.

Acoustic
(i) The sound characteristics of a room.
(ii) Any instrument designed for use without an amplifier.

Action
The height of the strings from the fretboard or neck of a stringed instrument, especially the guitar.

Ad lib.
(L) Improvise a section or repeat a phrase with extempore variations.

Adagio
(I) Lit. 'at ease'. Slow tempo - faster than Largo, slower than Andante.

ADT
Automatic Double Tracking. Recording technique used to thicken a vocal line or instrument. The part is re-recorded onto an adjacent track, with a slightly different echo or other effect, to create the illusion of two voices or instruments.

Aeolian
One of seven Greek scales, the Aeolian **mode** is the **interval** sequence A B C D E F G A. Also known as the 'natural minor' **scale**.

Air

A term that occurs initially in French and English music in the C16th to describe a **melody** or song. It is found in the music of Dowland, Campion and Purcell.

Allegro

(I) Lit. 'cheerful'. Lively, quick tempo. Allegretto is slightly slower than allegro.

Allemande

A popular Baroque dance, also known as an 'alman', which in the C16th formed part of the **Suite**'s structure.

Altered chord

A **chord** in which a note or notes are changed chromatically. Thus, the **chord** C7(♭5) (C E G♭ B♭) has had the fifth (G) flattened by a **semitone**.

Alto

(I) Lit. 'high'. High male or low female voice part spanning from G at the top of the bass clef to the C above **middle C**.

Ambient

Term popular in the 1990s to describe electronic music which has a dreamy atmosphere assisted by extensive use of **reverb** in the mix. Main proponents include The Orb and Aphex Twin.

Anacrusis

Term to describe an unstressed note or notes at the start of a piece of music or phrase.

Andante

(I) Lit. 'going'. At a moderate **tempo**, or walking pace. Between allegretto and **adagio.**

Animato

(I) Played in a lively, spirited manner.

Anticipation

Playing a note slightly early, or generally describing an effect of **syncopation**.

Antiphonal

An arrangement in which a piece of music uses two groups of performers to generate a 'call-and-response' structure.

Anthem

Choral composition deriving from the Latin motet, written for performance in church. Usually, but not necessarily, accompanied by organ.

A. O. R.

Adult Oriented Rock. Mildly derogatory term for a type of commercial rock music chiefly popular in the U.S. during the 1970s and 1980s and played by groups such as Fleetwood Mac, Boston, Foreigner, etc. See also **M. O. R.**

Appoggiatura

(I) 'leaning note'. A type of grace-note which creates a brief dissonance before resolving down to the next note. The appoggiatura is usually a tone or **semitone** above the main note.

Augmented

The augmented **triad** (C E G♯) is comprised of two major thirds. Also used of a note which has been sharpened within a **chord**: C7 (C E G B♭) becomes C7aug (C E G♯ B♭).

Aria

(I) 'style or manner'. A song or song-like piece associated with opera, usually in three sections, A.B.A. If the middle section is omitted, an arietta.

Arpeggio

Figure in which the notes of a **chord** are played one after the other rather than simultaneously.

Atonality

Music written without the organising principle of **keys**, **scales** and **harmony**.

B

Backing track

Piece of music used for singing over, and as such an instrumental mix of a song. This is also the meaning when the term is used in a recording studio. These have been popularised through karaoke machines. Backing tracks are also frequently used for performers to mime with on TV appearances.

Backline

The amplifiers arranged at the back of the stage for individual musicians. Contrasts with the monitor / **foldback** system and the P.A.

Backward guitar

Recording technique popularised in the 1960s. Reels of tape are taken off a reel-to-reel tape recorder and reversed. The guitarist then solos in the appropriate section, starting where the solo is meant to end and ending where the solo will start. When the tape is put back the right way, the notes are reversed, coming in quietly then suddenly cutting off.

Ballad/Ballade

A song telling a story in which each verse is set to the same music. The Ballade is a romantic piece for a single instrument, a title used by composers like Brahms and Schumann.

Bar

Line placed across the **stave** that divides music into rhythmic sections. The first beat of each **bar** always carries slightly more emphasis.

Barre

(F) Fretting technique on the guitar where a finger (usually the first) is laid flat on the neck to hold down more than one string.

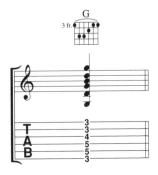

Baritone

Lit. 'Deep-sounding'. A **bass** voice of medium-low pitch, spanning from the F♯ above **middle C** down nearly two octaves to A.

Baroque

European music of the period 1600-1750, notable composers include J.S. Bach, Vivaldi, Purcell, Corelli, Handel and Scarlatti.

Bass

(i) Lowest part of a musical composition, significant for stabilising and defining the **harmony**.
(ii) Male voice part spanning F below the bass clef to D above **middle C**.

Bass drum

Along with the snare, the most important part of the drum kit, supplying a low frequency 'thud' which is offset by the higher frequency 'crack' of the snare. Most drum patterns in popular music are characterised by a variety of subtle patterns of the two.

Bass guitar

Devised in the 1950s as a convenient alternative to the double bass, the bass guitar has the same notes as the lower four strings of the guitar (EADG), but an octave lower. The electric bass is a vital part of the rhythm section in popular music. Acoustic bass guitars are also sometimes used.

Beatbox

(Colloq.) Electronic drum machine used in modern dance music.

Bend

A smooth change in pitch, usually up by a half or whole step, used on guitar, harmonica, and synthesiser.

Bi-amping

Form of amplification using sophisticated equipment that allows specific frequencies to be sent to more than one speaker according to which speaker is designed for which frequency. This is contrast to traditional amp/speaker configurations where a single type of speaker has to convey the whole signal.

Binary form

The balanced halves of a dance movement.

Bitonality

The use of two different **keys** at the same time.

Black note

The five black keys of the piano - C# D#
F# G# A# and their respective flats, D♭ E♭
G♭ A♭ and B♭.

Blue note

Harmonic effect crucial to **blues** or
blues-derived music. The singer or
soloist deliberately pitches a note a
semitone flat for the **key**, creating the
moody tension typical of the **blues**. The
commonest blue notes are the flattened
3rd and flattened 7th - in C major (C D
E F G A B C) E♭ and B♭.

Blues

Popular Afro-American vocal and
instrumental music with emotional roots
in the black experience of social
oppression. It began as a rural music in
the Mississippi delta, the first recordings
dating back to the 1920s. The migration
of many blacks to northern cities led to
the development of an urban, electric
blues typified by Muddy Waters and
Howlin' Wolf. The constituent parts of
blues music are extremely simple yet
capable of bearing the imprint of a host
of individual voices. The main forms are
8, 12, 16 or 32 bars, using **chords** I, IV
and V, often as **dominant** 7s. The
melodic content exhibits the use of the
flattened 3rd, 5th and 7th of the **scale**,
these notes deliberately clashing with
the major tonality underneath. Blues
enjoyed a significant revival in the
1960s when British rock musicians such
as Eric Clapton and John Mayall
introduced it to a wider audience by
recording blues songs and appearing
with the likes of John Lee Hooker,
Howlin' Wolf and B. B. King.

Bolero

Type of Spanish dance in triple time
now forever associated with the languid
modal **melody** and the strident,
obsessive rhythms of Ravel's
composition and in rock music with
'*Beck's Bolero*' (1968) by guitarists Jeff
Beck and Jimmy Page.

Boogie-woogie

Type of rhythmic **blues** popular in the
mid-C20th, chiefly for piano. The right
hand is free to improvise phrases while
the left hand maintains steady, repeating
bass figures often built on **dominant**
7th **arpeggios**.

Bootleg

Unofficial recording (usually of a concert), circulated in cassette, vinyl or CD format. Despite their illegality, the legendary status of bootlegs has done much to stimulate interest in major performers and to sustain their presence in popular music long after the act in question has split up. Possibly the most famous bootleg of all time was a recording of Bob Dylan's 1966 concert at the Manchester Free Trade Hall, entitled (confusingly) *Live At The Royal Albert Hall*. Should not be confused with piracy which is the counterfeiting of officially released product.

Bottleneck

Metal or glass tube placed on the third or fourth finger of the fretting hand, used by guitarists to produce distinctive **glissando** and **vibrato** effects. Altered tunings often assist the **slide** technique, which is heard in **blues**, rock and folk music.

Bouncing

Also known as 'ping-ponging'. Technique by which a recording on, say, track 1 is re-recorded ('bounced') onto another track, sometimes as another part is added. Bounces can be single (track 1 to track 2) or multiple (tracks 1-7 onto 8), and anything in between.

Bourrée

(F) Type of French dance similar to the **Gavotte** but taken at a quicker **tempo**, in 2/2 time and starting on the last crotchet of the **bar**.

B. P. M.

Beats Per Minute. Standardised tempo indication. Indicated by a crotchet, e.g. [♩] = 120 b.p.m.

Bridge

(i) Transitional section of a song connecting verse and **chorus**, sometimes having a similar function to a middle 8.
(ii) In instruments like the guitar and violin the piece of wood or metal over which the strings pass to the neck.

Broken chord

Accompaniment half way between **arpeggios** and **chord** playing. The **chords** are split up - often the root note is played first followed by the 3rd and 5th together - and unlike an **arpeggio** remain within one **octave**.

Bossa Nova

Lit. 'New Trend'; a popular Brazilian dance. Rhythm usually characterised by syncopation.

C

Cadence
(L) Lit. 'To fall' . A **chord** change which marks the end of a phrase in traditional **harmony**. There are four main types of cadence - **perfect**, **imperfect**, **plagal**, and **interrupted**.

Cadenza
Passage that occurs toward the conclusion of a **concerto** movement designed to exhibit the technical brilliance of the solo featured performer.

Calypso
Dance form with its origins in West Indian folk music, associated with Trinidad and the Caribbean.

Canon
Music in which several voices sing the same melodic line but begin and end at different times. Unlike a **round**, the second voice can enter before the first has finished its phrase, and may be transposed down or up a 4th or 5th.

Cantabile
(I) In a singing style.

Cantata
A piece of music composed for solo voices, **chorus** and **orchestra**. During the **Baroque** era it was a piece of sacred music but eventually also developed secular themes.

Capo D'astro
Abbrev. Capo. Device that wraps around a guitar neck, raising the pitch of the strings. Allows playing in difficult **keys** or in keys that suit a singer's voice, and changes the tone of the guitar making unique **chord** voicings possible high up the neck.

Catch
Tune with four phrases which can be sung simultaneously without discord. The catch is started one phrase at a time until all four are going. Examples include 'London's Burning' or 'Frère Jacques'.

Chamber music
Music written not for the concert hall but for more intimate surroundings. A typical chamber ensemble is the **string quartet**.

Chorale
Hymn-tune, most famously associated with J. S. Bach. Generations of students have learned **harmony** by fitting **chords** to Bach chorale melodies.

Chord

Group of more than two notes played together, in contrast to an **interval** which consists of only two notes. Chords produce **harmony**, in contrast to the rhythmic and melodic components of music.

Chorus

(i) In **classical** music, singers supplying vocal sections in a longer work.
(ii) In popular music, the most memorable section of a song, often repeated.
(iii) Electronic **delay** effect that slightly alters pitch of original signal, creating a distinctive thickening of the sound.

Chromatic

A note or **chord** which does not normally occur within the **key**. Thus in C major the notes C♯, D♯, F♯, G♯ and A♯ are all chromatic. Chromaticism is the extensive use of such notes or chords to extend the **harmony**.

Circle of fifths

Progression of the **keys** in a circle. Starting at C major, the major **keys** progress by fifths (3 1/2 tones) to G, D, A, E, B, F♯, C♯. B is also C♭, F♯ is G♭, C# is Db, and continuing in fifths gives A♭, E♭, B, F and finally C, thus completing the circle.

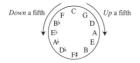

Classical

Term used popularly and imprecisely of any music classified as 'high culture' or 'serious', played on traditional orchestral instruments from written parts. More correctly, European music of the mid-eighteenth century to the early C19th, typified by Mozart, Haydn and early Beethoven.

Music from the Classical period has a well-defined **harmony** and strong interest in maintaining and establishing formal rules of composition.

Clef

(F) key. A sign placed on the **stave** to fix the pitch of the lines. The G treble clef fixes the second line as G, the F bass clef fixes the fourth line as F. There are also C alto clefs and tenor clefs.

Treble clef   Alto clef   Bass clef

Click bass

Popular electric bass style of the late 1960s / early 1970s defined both by tone - a trebly sound and the use of a pick - and stylistically by an imitation of the eighth-note **syncopation** of the **Motown** bassist James Jamerson.

Coda

Lit. 'tail'. The final section of a piece of music culminating in the last **bar**.

Compact Disc
(CD). Digital recording format on which information stored on a disk is read by a laser.

Common time
Another term for 4/4 time, four crotchet beats in a bar.

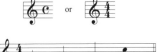

Comping
(Colloq.) Providing a simple chordal accompaniment to a soloist. Also known as vamping.

Compound interval
Distance between two notes greater than an **octave**. A major **ninth** is the compound version of a major 2nd.

Major 2nd   Major 9th

Compound Time
A time-signature in which the basic pulse or beat is divisible by three. E.g: 6/8, 9/8, 12/8. See also **simple time** and **duple time**.

Compression
Sound effect used in recordings to increase the volume of quieter sounds and limit louder ones so as to prevent peak signals which would otherwise spoil a recording.

Concert pitch
Universal reference in which the note A is taken as having a **frequency** of 440Hz.

Concerto
Large-scale concert work in three movements usually featuring **orchestra** and a solo instrument.

Consonance
Combinations of notes pleasing to the ear. The **intervals** of major and minor 3rd and 6th are consonant. Opposite of **dissonance**.

Contrary motion
Effect caused by two melodic lines moving in opposite directions. Contrasts with oblique motion where one voice remains on the same note while the other moves.

Contrapuntal
Music in which several melodic lines move independently of each other yet still sustain a sense of harmonic organisation in terms of the **chords** they produce or imply. Counterpoint is a more rigidly defined type of contrapuntal music, having specific rules governing the movement of the different parts.

Counter-tenor

Lit. 'Against the tenor'. The highest male voice, not to be confused with male alto or falsetto.

Crescendo

Direction for music to increase in volume.

Crosstalk

Unwanted sound heard on analogue **multi-track** recordings where, owing to the existence of parallel tracks on tape, some of the signal on one track can be heard on an adjacent track at high volume or during very quiet passages.

Crotchet

Quarter-note, four of which make a **bar** of 4/4 time.

Cutaway

Contouring of the guitar-body to make notes on the high frets more accessible easily. The Gibson Les Paul is a single cutaway guitar, the Fender Stratocaster a double cutaway.

Examples of cutaway:

Fender Stratocaster - double cutaway

Gibson Les Paul - single cutaway

D

Da capo al fine
(I) Return to the beginning and play through until the end.

Dal segno al fine
(I) Return to the dal segno sign (*D.S.*) and play through to the end.

D.A.T.
Digital Audio Tape. Trademarked name for a type of audio tape on which digital information can be stored on two tracks.

Decibel
Abbrev. dB. A unit for measuring relative levels of power, voltage and sound intensity, and hence an objective indication of loudness.

Delay
Effect originally called 'echo', in which a note or sound is recorded and then played back at differing volumes to the original note.

Demo
Composer's initial recording, not intended for release, sometimes recorded quickly and with limited arrangement, for personal reference or to attract the interest of music publishers or companies.

Development
Technique in **classical** music whereby a musical idea is extended and changed, essential to longer works such as concertos and symphonies.

Diatonic
Intervals or **chords** derived from notes in or related to the tonic scale, in contrast to **chromatic**.

Diminished
Opposite to **augmented**. Refers to any **triad**, e.g. C E♭ G♭ in which the **intervals** are two minor 3rds. If a further note is added B♭♭ (A) another minor 3rd up, the diminished 7th **chord** is formed. The diminished **triad** naturally occurs as **chord** VII in a major **key** (in C major, B D F).

Diminuendo
Direction for music to get quieter in volume.

Dirge
General term for any slow piece of a mournful nature, especially connected with death and funerals.

Disco

Style of singles-oriented dance music popular in the mid-70s, celebrated in the film Saturday Night Fever. Disco is typified by a four-to-the-**bar** bass drum beat and pronounced eighth-note, or quaver, octaves in the bass.

Disjunct motion

A musical phrase that moves in leaps rather than in steps.

Dissonance

Opposite of **consonance**. A dissonance is a sound which is traditionally perceived as not harmonious. The minor **second** C-C♯, augmented 4th C-F♯ and major 7th C-B are dissonant **intervals**.

C-B

Dominant

The fifth note and **chord** of the **major scale**.

Dominant (G)
Chord of G

Dorian

One of the seven Greek **modes** or scales, the Dorian **mode** is the **interval** sequence D E F G A B C D (a natural minor scale with a raised 6th).

D   E   F   G   A   B   C   D

Dot

A dot placed after a note increases the duration of that note by 50%. A dotted **crotchet** [♩.] is therefore a **crotchet** plus a **quaver**. Similarly, a double dot increases the duration of the note by half plus a quarter, therefore a double-dotted **minim** equals a **minim**, plus a **crotchet**, plus a **quaver**.

Downbeat

The first beat of the **bar**, and also the third beat in 4/4. It contrasts with the upbeat (beats 2 and 4) and the off-beat which in 4/4 is represented by even numbered eighth notes.

Drone

Note or group of notes played repeatedly to support a **melody** or changing **chords**. Drones are often found in non-Western music, especially those which have an emphasis on **melody** but not on **harmony**.

Drop-in

Recording technique for correcting mistakes. The musician plays along with the recorded part and the engineer starts recording at the moment where the mistake occurred. Once the musician has supplied the correct notes, the engineer cancels the record mode.

Dry
An original sound signal without any effects processing (such as **reverb**). Contrasts with **wet**.

Duple time
2/4 time or two beats in a **bar**. See also **compound** and **simple** time.

Dynamics
The understanding and use of volume in music, contrasting loud and quiet passages. e.g:

p = soft (piano)

f = loud (forte)

mf = moderately loud (mezzoforte)

Early Music
Term that describes both a period and an attitude towards the interpretation and performance of music. Generally means music up to about 1650, especially those composers and works neglected because their music was written for obsolete instruments such as the lute and viol. It became popular to play this music with the greatest possible authenticity, using faithful reproductions of antique instruments and attempting to expunge from performance any assumptions about expression which were the product of later centuries.

E-bow
Battery-powered device held in a guitarist's picking hand which causes the string to produce an endlessly sustained note.

Effects unit
Electrical circuit, analogue or digital, designed to modify sound. They range from small, single-effect units turned on and off with footswitches, to complex multi-parameter programmable modules. Used with most electric instruments, though when used as part of the recording / mixing process, they can alter the sound of instruments with an acoustic source.

Electric guitar
Version of the classical (Spanish) and steel-strung acoustic instrument which relies on magnetic pickups for much of its sound. The vibrating strings create fluctuations in the magnetic field which in turn are converted into an electric signal strengthened by an amplifier and so rendered audible by a speaker. The electric guitar can be solid or semi-solid. It is tuned in the same manner as the acoustic guitar, although it tends to be strung with lighter gauge strings. Very few instruments have the potential to move as much air and generate as much sound as the electric guitar. Marketed at first almost as a toy, it has staked a claim to be the quintessential instrument of the twentieth century.

Electro-acoustic
Type of acoustic guitar developed in the 1970s-80s to get round the problem of amplifying through a microphone in a concert. The electro-acoustic has a built-in pickup and usually some form of volume and tone controls to enable the sound of the guitar to pass direct into an amplifier or P.A. Recently, nylon-strung examples have appeared.

Enharmonic
In certain musical situations such as a key-change, a note can change its name without changing its pitch. In a key-change from E minor to E♭ major, the D♯ of E minor becomes E♭ of the new **key**. This is an enharmonic change.

Enhancer
Sound processing unit found in studios
designed to add extra overall 'sparkle' to
a **mix**, or to give one instrument greater
prominence.

Equal temperament
A tuning system based on dividing the
octave into twelve equal parts. See
temperament.

Equalisation
Abbrev. E.Q. Mixing process either
during recording or at a live concert
where different frequencies can be cut
or boosted, to set the tonal balance.

Étude
(Fr. 'Study'). A piece of variable form
designed to allow the performer or
student to exercise an aspect of
technique.

Exposition
Initial statement of a musical theme
which is then subject to **development**.

Fader
Sliding control on a mixing desk or similar by which a signal's level is increased or reduced.

Falsetto
Type of singing used by male vocalists to extend the upward range of their voices. The falsetto voice uses only part of the vocal chords and is therefore weaker than the normal voice. It can produce delicate, expressive and shrill effects.

Fanfare
Short piece of music usually played on brass instruments at a ceremonial occasion. More generally understood to be the introduction to, or homage to, a person or event.

Feedback
Noise created when an amplified note is fed back into the electrical system which produced it in the first place. This causes the note to sustain, increase in volume and often 'decay' into one of its higher **harmonics**.

Flam
Technique used by drummers in which the snare drum is struck by both sticks a fraction of a second apart, creating a dramatic effect.

Flamenco
Popular folk-music of Spain, featuring dancing and a **virtuoso** guitar technique combining vigorous strumming, percussive tapping of the guitar body, and **Phrygian** melodies.

Figured bass
Notation system by which numbers written in the **bass** indicate the type of **chord** intended to harmonise that bass note.

Finale
Last movement of a longer piece of music with several movements.

Fine
(I) Lit. 'the end'.

Fingering
Process of interpretation in which an instrumentalist chooses which fingers to use to play each note in a piece in order to produce the best performance.

Flanging
Sound effect used on electric guitar involving a moving sweep of frequencies (similar to phasing).

Flat
Accidental placed in front of a note, lowering it by a **semitone**.

Foldback
Arrangement of speakers at the front and side of a stage which projects sound back to the performers, enabling them to hear themselves.

Folk Baroque
Term coined to describe the ornate fingerstyle of 1960s folk guitarists such as John Renbourn, Bert Jansch and Davey Graham.

Folk music
Term which covers an enormous variety of music but which is generally understood to be 'of the people' and tends therefore to be defined against 'high' or 'serious' music. Folk music in its traditional form is a body of music - songs, melodies, dances and lyrics - which expresses the sensibility and experiences of the mass of a population using acoustic, low-tech instruments and a relatively simple musical aesthetic of form and harmony. Interest in folk melodies has been shown from time to time by 'serious' composers. There was a revival of folk music after World War II. Some would argue that commercial pop, rock and soul has superseded the folk music of the twentieth century.

Folk rock
Hybrid of Anglo-American folk music developed in the 1960s. It involves the arrangement of traditional material for variations on the rock line-up of acoustic and electric guitar, bass and drums, with electric violin and mandolin sometimes present. The chief exponents include Fairport Convention and Steeleye Span in the UK, Alan Stivell in France, and The Byrds in the US. The term is more loosely applied to rock music with a softer, more acoustic approach.

Forte
(1) Play loudly.

Fortepiano
(i) Successor to the harpsichord and forerunner of the modern 'grand' piano.
(ii) As a playing direction, means to play loudly then quietly.

Frequency
Pitch is measured by the number of cycles per second. One Hertz equals one cycle per second. **Middle C** is 256 Hz.

Fret
A thin piece of metal, wood or ivory laid across and hammered into a fingerboard which marks the place where the finger is placed to produce a note of that pitch. Frets are found on instruments such as the guitar, mandolin and banjo. 'To fret' means to hold down a note on such a fingerboard.

Fretless bass
Type of electric bass guitar with the frets removed, facilitating pitch-smooth glissandos and similar expressive effects. The sound was popularised by Jaco Pastorius in the 1970s.

Fugue
Complex **baroque** work usually for keyboard involving the statement and **development** of musical themes which overlap in a precise manner. The most famous examples are Bach's Forty-Eight Preludes and Fugues.

Fundamental note
The most important **frequency** in a note, in contrast to the **overtones** which are also present but not as audible.

Funk
Originally used in the 1950s among jazz musicians, the term is now associated with a sub-genre of commercial black music developed out of R'n'B by James Brown in the 1960s and popularised in the 1970s. This is an earthy, street-wise form of soul, with strong bass and rhythms, especially an emphasis on the first down beat of the bar, and 'looped' motifs.

FX
Abbrev. for sound effects.

G

Gain
Control on a studio mixing desk which increases the input level on that channel. On small guitar amplifiers this increases the distortion.

Galliard
A popular sixteenth century dance, usually lively and in 3/4 time. The name was also used for pieces played on instruments such as the Elizabethan Galliard.

Garage band
Term to describe a primitive style of rock music, usually played by a guitar/bass/drums line-up, consisting of loud, fast, short songs with no pretensions to be 'art' but manifesting instead a 'trash' aesthetic. It derives from the U.S. and from the necessity of amateur bands with no money to practise in garages. The earliest garage bands date from the 1960s.

Gavotte
C18th French dance-form in 2/2 time exhibiting four-**bar** phrases which often start in the middle of the **bar**, and a lively **tempo**.

Gig
Colloquial expression for a concert or similar musical performance.

Giusto
(It.) Meaning precise or exact, normally met with in the phrase 'tempo giusto', telling the performer to keep the time strict.

Glam rock
Singles-oriented music popular in the UK from 1971-74, typified by David Bowie, T. Rex, and Roxy Music. Glam rejected both the musical pretentions of progressive rock and the introspection of the singer-songwriters. It revived some musical traits of 1950s rock'n'roll and dressed them up in space-age androgyny.

Glissando
An ascending or descending **slur** of notes progressing in a continuous raising or lowering of pitch.

gliss.

Glued-neck
Element of electric guitar construction where the neck is glued into place, in contrast to the 'bolt-on' design. The Gibson Les Paul has a glued-neck, the Fender Stratocaster a bolt-on neck.

Grace-notes
Notes added to the main note to add
musical interest, including the
acciaccatura, **appoggiatura**, mordent
and trill.

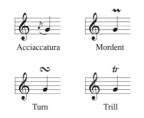

Acciaccatura	Mordent

Turn	Trill

Gospel
Influential style of Afro-American vocal
music originally sung by black
congregations during church services,
unaccompanied or with clapping or
minimal instrumental accompaniment
from piano or organ. The vocal style is
blues-influenced, impassioned and
communitarian in ethic, allowing
individual voices to decorate short
phrases at will. Call-and-response
techniques also feature. Gospel was a
vital part of 1960s soul music as can be
heard in the recordings of artists such as
Aretha Franklin and the Edwin Hawkins
singers.

Graphic Equaliser
Or 'Graphic E.Q.': a sound processing
unit that enables very fine adjustments
to be made to different frequencies.
These are divided into a number of
'bands'.

Gregorian chant
Early form of Western sacred vocal
music named after Pope Gregory (590-
604AD) utilising unaccompanied unison
singing in an accentless free time.

Groove
Slang expression in popular music to
describe the subtler rhythms in a song or
piece of music. It refers to the human
'feel' element in a performance, in
particular slight anticipations and
delaying of the beat. The word is
invariably approving.

Grunge
Style of rock music which enjoyed
considerable success in the early 1990s,
arising from the Seattle music scene and
exemplified by the band Nirvana.
Grunge took the **riffs** of heavy rock but
replaced its guitar **virtuoso** ethos with
the anarchic mentality of **punk**. Almost
single-handedly this created a revolution
in US rock, but Grunge never recovered
from the death of Kurt Cobain,
Nirvana's singer/guitarist, in April 1994.

Half-note
U.S. term for a **minim** or two-beat note in **simple time**.

Harmonics
Generally these are **overtones** which form part of a note, sounding above the **fundamental**. More specifically, 'ghost' notes that can be found at certain points along a string. See **Fundamental**.

Harmony
(i) The underlying **chord** structures of a piece of music usually based in a chosen **key** or mixture of keys.
(ii) In a vocal context the addition of backing voices to a **melody**, often a third or sixth away from the **melody** note.

Harmonisation
The process of taking a melodic line and adding **chords** to it.

Heavy Metal
Style of rock music in 1980s which evolved from late 60s hard / heavy rock, exemplified by bands such as Iron Maiden, AC/DC and Metallica. 'HM' features repetitive slogging beats and low-pitched guitar phrases (**riffs**), frequent and extensive guitar solos and growled vocals, with morbid lyrics focusing on death and destruction.

Heavy Rock
Style of rock which developed out of the high volume rock / blues of the 1967-69 period. Songs came to be structured around repeated guitar figures played at a low pitch and often constructed from the pentatonic minor and blues scales. High volume levels and increasing stretches of guitar soloing encouraged vocalists to pitch ever higher in an effort to compete and use the voice as another instrument. Powerful drumming was another factor. Heavy rock is in some ways the less pretentious side of progressive rock. Typical bands include Led Zeppelin, Deep Purple and Black Sabbath.

Hexachord
Not actually a chord but a scale consisting of the first six notes of the major scale (in C major: C D E F G A).

Hi-hat
Part of a drum-kit, the hi-hat is a foot-operated unit consisting of two matched cymbals facing each other which can be opened and closed, and played with a stick. The hi-hat serves an important background time-keeping function, since it is often played to generate a continuous stream of eighth notes.

Hip-hop

Form of popular black music which developed out of the clubs of New York in the late 1980s in which the DJ becomes an ersatz musician 'playing' a multi-deck turntable, and manually manipulating vinyl records ('scratching'). Drum-loops, rapping, and improvisation are other elements of this dance music.

Home triad

Another expression for the key chord.

Hook

(*Colloq.*) Expression in popular songwriting for the melodic, lyric or harmonic idea most likely to imprint itself on a listener after hearing it only once or twice.

Humbucker

Type of **pick-up** for the electric guitar developed in the 1950s with two magnetic coils (hence 'double-coil') which 'buck the hum' endemic to single coil **pick-ups**. Humbuckers are quieter than single coils and have a thicker, less trebly tone.

Hungarian Scale

The harmonic minor scale with an augmented fourth. In C: C D E♭ F♯ G A♭ B C. The presence of two leaps of 1½ tones (3-4, 6-7) gives the scale an exotic sound.

C   D   E♭   F♯   G   A♭   B   C

I

Imperfect cadence
The presence of **chords** I to V at the end of a musical phrase, creating a mood of expectancy.

```
I  -  V
G     D
```

Impromptu
Not an improvised piece but rather one characterised by impulsiveness, a title used by such C19th composers as Schumann, Chopin, Mendelssohn and Liszt.

Intelligent
Used of sound effect units, notably harmonisers, able to imitate certain musical processes. Early harmonisers for voice or guitar developed in the 1970s would add a major 3rd above every note regardless of the requirements of the **major scale**. An intelligent harmoniser will adjust to a minor or a major 3rd, depending on which is correct.

Intonation
The determining of whether a note is

true to pitch. On fretted instruments such as the guitar, intonation indicates whether adjustment to the neck is necessary to make notes in tune anywhere on the neck.

Interrupted cadence
A **chord** change which suggests a **perfect cadence** (V-I) and instead creates surprise by going from V to another **chord**, often VI.

```
V  -  VI
D     Em
```

Interval
Distance between two notes. The intervals of the **major scale** are: major 2nd, major 3rd, **perfect 4th**, **perfect 5th**, major 6th, major 7th, and an **octave**.

C major

Inversion
A simple **triad** such as C major or minor (C E G / C E♭ G) can have three forms: **root position** (where C is the

bass note), first inversion (where E or
E♭ is the **bass** note) or second inversion
(where G is the **bass** note). **Root
position chords** sound stable, first
inversions are mobile and emphasise
their tonality, whereas second inversions
are unstable.

C minor

Root   1st   2nd
         inversion   inversion

Ionian
One of the seven Greek **modes** or
scales, the Ionian **mode** is the **interval**
sequence C D E F G A B C . Also
known as the **major scale**.

I.P.S.
Abbrev. for 'inches per second',
governing the speed of tape machines.

Jam
(Verb) 1960s/70s popular music slang expression for improvising. The Grateful Dead and Cream were two rock acts famous for on-stage jamming. The term also became the title of a famous Bob Marley song.

Jangle guitar
Style of electric guitar playing used in pop and less 'heavy' rock. The style is rhythmic and arpeggiated, exploiting the guitar's capacity for chord voicings in which notes are doubled at the same pitch. The historical origins of 'jangle guitar' lie in the playing of George Harrison of The Beatles and Roger McGuinn of The Byrds, both of whom played the Rickenbacker electric 12-string.

Jazz
Popular Afro-American music with roots in the **blues**. Initially heard as the New Orleans jazz of the 20s and 30s, it later underwent many stylistic changes establishing a range of sub-genres from 'trad jazz' to free-form, avante-garde jazz, including the big band Dixieland Revival of the 1940s, and hybrids such as jazz-funk. Jazz has a complex **harmony**, uses **swing rhythm** and **blue notes**, and places a stronger emphasis on **development** than other popular music, especially through improvisation.

Jazz-rock
Fusion of jazz and rock styles initiated from the jazz field in the mid-60s as jazz attempted to emulate some of the commercial success of rock. Notable exponents included Miles Davis, Herbie Hancock and Keith Jarrett.

Jingle
Catchy short piece of instrumental or vocal music - sometimes no more than a few seconds - used for advertising purposes.

Jug band
Small group of musicians using improvised instruments drawn from the domestic environment, such as tea-chest bass, washboard, washtub, spoons, coupled with acoustic guitar and harmonica, to play simple, infectious modern folk songs. Arising from an attempt to make the best of austere conditions, the jug band ethos clearly had an influence on skiffle.

Jumbo
Term applied to an extra large-bodied acoustic guitar. The most famous model is probably that made by Gibson, the J-200, designed in the late 1930s.

Jungle
Sub-genre of 1990s dance music, played on electronic keyboards and drum machines, featuring a stripped down and brutally rhythmic sound. Grew out of **hip-hop**, and consists primarily of speeded-up breakbeats, hence its other commonly used title, drum'n'bass.

Key

Sense of tonality which governs music, created by a scale and its **chords**. The C **major scale** C D E F G A B C generates the **chords** C Dm Em F G Am and B dim. A piece in C major creates a sense of key in which the key-note C and its chord subjectively feel like the centre around which everything is organised. There is aesthetic pleasure each time this 'home' chord is reached and an awareness of journeying away from it when the **harmony** moves to other **chords**. All major keys have identical internal relationships. As such, heard in isolation, they are identical, merely pitched higher or lower. However, heard in relation to each other in a key-change they create strong contrasts and a more powerful feeling of journeying. See **modulation**.

Key relationship

Keys with a similar number of sharps or flats to the 'home' key are regarded as near; those with a radically different number are distant. Thus F major, G major and A minor are all near keys for C major; D♭major, F♯major and G♯ minor are distant.

Key signature

Arrangement of accidentals at the beginning of a piece indicating the 'key' to the performer. There are 15 key signatures: seven **sharp**, seven **flat** and C major which has no **sharps** or **flats**.

A Major   B♭ Major

Kick drum

Another name for bass drum, so-called because it is played by the drummer's foot pressing down on a pedal.

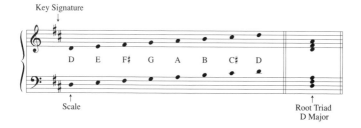

Key Signature

D E F♯ G A B C♯ D

Scale   Root Triad
                        D Major

Koto

Japanese zither-like instrument with a rectangular body, usually 13 strings tuned in various pentatonic scales. The notes are fingered with the left hand, struck by the right. The koto is part of the traditional ensemble with the shamisen and shakuhachi.

Krautrock

Unfortunate but persistent label for certain types of rock emanating from Germany in the 1970s. The term is associated most with Can and Kraftwerk, and therefore implies some degree of experimentation and use of synthesizers.

L

Largo
(I) Slow and stately.

Lead guitar
In pop and **rock** music the guitar (usually electric) that counterpoints the vocal **melody** and provides solos. Brought to prominence in the 1960s British **Blues** boom and by the first generation of **rock** guitar virtuosi - Eric Clapton, Jeff Beck, Jimmy Page, Jimi Hendrix, Carlos Santana, etc.

Leading note
The 7th note of the scale, in many scales a **semitone** away from the **octave**.

Leakage
In the studio, instruments are traditionally 'isolated' so that each microphone only picks up the instrument in front of it and not others playing nearby. High volumes, such as generated by rock bands, can cause leakage of one instrument into another instrument's microphone.

Legato
(I) To play smoothly.

Leger line
Sometimes spelt 'ledger'. Small line added to facilitate the writing of a note above or below the **stave**.

Leitmotif
(G) 'leading motif'. The use of a repeated phrase or musical idea throughout a longer piece to symbolise a person, an object or an idea. Especially significant in the works of Wagner.

Leslie effect
Sound created by feeding a signal through a Leslie speaker revolving at high speed causing pitch fluctuations in the note. Most commonly used for keyboard and guitar. The **bridge** section of Cream's 'Badge' (1969) illustrates the sound of a guitar fed through a Leslie.

Libretto
The words for an opera or musical, originally printed as a small book for the audience to read during the performance.

Lick
Slang term used mostly in pop/rock music, to describe a short musical phrase which many be repeated often during the song.

Liturgy
The text of a Christian service set to music.

Locrian

One of the seven Greek **modes** or scales, the Locrian mode is the **interval** sequence B C D E F G A B (a natural minor scale with a flattened 2nd and 5th).

Loop

Originally, a section of tape edited to repeat a sound for the length of a recording. In the 1960s The Beatles experimented with tape loops, using them to stunning effect on songs like 'Tomorrow Never Knows' and 'Being For The Benefit Of Mr Kite'. Digital technology has made looping an effortless procedure, either by programming or sampling.

Lullaby

A cradle-song.

Lute

Forerunner of the guitar, the lute was popular throughout Europe during the Middle Ages until the mid-C17th. The number of strings and body dimensions varied greatly, though common features include catgut frets, strings doubled at the same pitch, a curved-back body, and ornately decorated sound-holes. In the 1590s player-composers such as John Dowland developed a complex, contrapuntal style for the instrument.

Lydian

One of the seven Greek **modes** or scales, the Lydian mode is the **interval** sequence F G A B C D E F (a **major scale** with a raised 4th).

Lyric

(i) The words to a song.
(ii) Lyrical: to play in a melodious, 'singing' manner.

Madrigal
C16th unaccompanied piece, usually **contrapuntal** and secular in theme, to be sung by a small group of voices in a domestic setting.

Maestoso
(I) 'Majestically'.

Mainstream
Music generally agreed to be of a current trend.

Major interval
Two notes which are a tone, two tones, $2^1/_2$, $3^1/_2$, or $4^1/_2$ tones apart defined in relation to the **major scale**.

Major 3rd   Major 6th

Major scale
Pattern of notes arranged according to the **interval** sequence Tone-Tone-Semitone-Tone-Tone-Tone-Semitone.

D Major

- tone - tone - semitone - tone - tone - tone - semitone -

Measure
U.S. expression for a **bar**.

Mediant
The **third** note of the scale.

Medley
Practice of combining extracts from several songs or pieces into one continuous performance, sometimes with the object of enabling more popular tunes to be heard in the limited time of a concert.

Melisma
(i) A group of notes sung to one syllable.
(ii) Elaborate decoration of a **melody** by a singer intended to intensify the emotion but often merely showcasing the singer's technique. Typical of black music styles such as **soul**, **rhythm'n'blues** and **gospel**.

Melody
Sequence of single notes, either sung or played by an instrument, which are the focus of interest.

Melodic minor scale

Scale created when the sixth and 7th notes of the natural minor scale are raised and then restored to their normal pitch coming down. The fixed melodic minor raises these notes both ascending and descending.

C minor

Natural

Mellotron

1960s keyboard designed to imitate strings, flutes and other orchestral instruments. Physically heavy and subject to tuning problems, the Mellotron has long since been superseded by digital synthesisers, but retains a reedy charm apparent on The Beatles' 'Strawberry Fields Forever' (1967) and The Moody Blues' 'Nights In White Satin' (1968).

Metronome

Electronic or spring-operated device for creating a regular rhythmic pulse at any **tempo**, enabling the player to practise to a steady beat.

Microtone

Pitch-**interval** smaller than a **semitone**. Microtones are used in non-Western musical traditions, some **rock** music, and avant-garde **classical** music.

Middle C

Note in or closest to the centre of a piano keyboard whose **frequency** is 256 Hz, written one **leger** line down from the treble **clef**.

Middle Eight

Section of a song that comes after the second **chorus** and acts as a **bridge** to either a solo, a verse or another **chorus**. Eight is a typical length but the term applies regardless of the number of bars.

MIDI

Musical Instrument Digital Interface. Revolutionary system by which digital instruments can 'talk' to one another and be linked for recording and live performance.

Minim

Also known as a Half-note; a note lasting two **crotchet** beats.

1 - 2   1 - 2

Minor interval
Interval of a **semitone**, $1^1/2$ tones, 4 or 5 tones defined in relation to the **minor scale**.

minor 3rd   minor 6th

Minor scale
The minor scale has three main forms. In A the natural minor runs A B C D E F G A; the harmonic minor is A B C D E F G♯ A; the **melodic minor** A B C D E F♯ G♯ A with the two **sharps** removed when descending.

Minuet
Popular dance form of the C17th and C18th in triple time.

Mix
(Verb): final stage in the recording process, where combined parts in a multitrack recording are balanced and additional effects added. The multitrack is then copied to a stereo recording, resulting in *(noun)* a mix. At a concert, the mix is the balance of instruments coming through the P.A.

Mixolydian
One of the seven Greek **modes** or scales, the Mixolydian **mode** is the **interval** sequence G A B C D E F G (a **major scale** with a flattened 7th). Since **blues** music often flattens the 7th, this scale is common in pop / **rock** music,

the resulting straight major **chord** VII replacing the less useful **diminished** VII of the **major scale** proper.

G   A   B   C   D   E   F   G

M. O. R.
Mildly derogatory acronym meaning 'middle of the road'. Highly commercial style of popular music which tends to erase any feature - rhythmic, harmonic or lyrical - which might cause offence or be startling. As such it is highly conservative and sentimental, tuneful at the expense of **rhythm**, harmonic invention, and lyrical meaning. The Carpenters were the classic M. O. R. band of the 1970s. See also **A. O. R.**

Mode
Scale originating in ancient Greece. There are 7 main modes: **Ionian, Dorian, Phrygian, Lydian, Mixolydian, Aeolian** and **Locrian**.

Moderato
(I) Played moderately.

Modulation
Key-change. Modulation is an essential feature of longer works to prevent monotony. Key-changes create significant contrasts of meaning and emotion, as the listener is moved from one tonal centre to another. Keys with a similar number of **sharps** or **flats** to the

'home' key are regarded as 'near'; those with a radically different number are 'distant'. Thus F major, G major and A minor are all near keys for C major; D♭ major, F♯ major and G♯ minor are distant.

Monitor
See **foldback**.

Motown
Short-hand for the popular **soul** music released on the Detroit Motown record label 1960-72. 'Classic' 1960s Motown was danceable, with a strong beat, sometimes four-to-the-bar snare drum, and highly commercial. Along with Atlantic and Stax, it was the most important label for black music in that period.

Multi-track
Type of recording (either on analogue tape or digital medium) in which musical parts are laid down side by side on a number of 'tracks'. During the first half of the 1960s multitrack recording was on 2, 3 or 4 track. The second half of the 1960s saw 8-track become the norm, quickly followed by 16, 24, 32 and 48 in the 1970s.

Musique concrete
Form of highbrow C20th experimental music concerned with creating collages of sound on tape.

Mute
Technique whereby the normal sound of an instrument is slightly damped or blocked, creating a different, less forceful sound. With a trumpet this is achieved by a hand-held plug which almost seals the hole; on the guitar muting is achieved by putting the side of the picking hand on the strings very near the **bridge** or tailpiece.

Nashville tuning
Guitar tuning in which the lower four strings E A D G are replaced with thinner strings so that they can be tuned an **octave** higher than usual.

String no:	6th	5th	4th	3rd	2nd	1st
Note name:	E	A	D	G	B	E

Natural
Type of **accidental** which cancels out the effect of a **sharp** or **flat**.

B flat   B natural

New Age music
New Age music has its roots in Brian Eno's ambient experiments; it aims for a remedial effect, promising to soothe the nerves and uplift the spirit by inducing tranquil, reflective states. Synth voices and approximations of ethnic instruments such as pan-pipes blend with string-sounds in washes of reverb. Rhythm or dissonance are reduced to a minimal role in favour of simplistic melodies and harmony. Typically, 'authentic' elements such as plainsong or folk melodies are combined with sophisticated electronica to create a contemplative and calming atmosphere.

New Romantic
Phase in popular music during the early 1980s typified by artists such as Soft Cell, Spandau Ballet, Duran Duran, The Human League, and Gary Numan. New Romantic music was typified by short, commercial songs and androgynous imagery but unlike glam rock rejected the hegemony of the guitar. Instead it embraced the new technology of early drum machines and synthesizers, with the consequence that much of it now sounds dated.

New Wave
New Wave was the second shock from the U.K. punk-rock explosion of 1976. It softened the political and anarchic aspects of punk, and made the songs more musical and therefore more commercial without relinquishing the no-nonsense get-to-the-point spirit. Unlike New Romantics, most New Wave was guitar oriented. Significant artists who surfed New Wave to success included Elvis Costello, Graham Parker, Television, The Police, Talking Heads and The Pretenders.

Nickleodeon

Early C20th mechanical device which generated music from a specially designed roll of paper on the insertion of a coin. Found in public places, these were superseded by the jukebox in the 1930s.

Ninth

Individually, the distance between the 1st note of the scale and the 2nd, one **octave** higher. The ninth **chord** includes the 1st, 3rd, 5th, ♭7th and 9th of the scale.

Interval   Chord

Nocturne

An instrumental piece of indeterminate form, usually with a dreamy night-time quality, popularised by the pianist / composer Chopin in the C19th.

Noise gate

Sound processing device which automatically silences ('gates') a channel when the incoming signal drops below a certain volume, thus preventing unwanted background noise.

Notation

Any method for writing music down on paper. Standard notation systems use the five-line **stave**. Some instruments such as the guitar have their own alternative which is used either alone or in conjunction with the traditional **stave**. See **tablature**.

Note-row

Term used in serial or twelve-tone music to describe a series of notes which are taken as the basis for an atonal composition – one not written according to traditional scales, keys or harmony.

Octave
The distance between any note and the same note 12 semitones higher or lower.

Octet
Composition for eight instruments.

Off-beat
In a bar of 4/4 the off-beat falls on the even-numbered eighth notes: 1 2 3 4 5 6 7 8. The odd-numbered notes carry the beat. The 2 and 4 quarter-note beats can also be treated in a similar fashion depending on tempo. Deliberate accenting of the off-beat is a hallmark of **reggae**.

Open score
The use of a separate **stave** for individual voices rather than combining onto one.

Open string
A string on an instrument such as the guitar or violin which is played without a finger on it. Open string notes have a different timbre - or sound quality - to fretted or fingered notes.

Open tuning
Guitar technique whereby standard EADGBE tuning is changed so that the open strings will produce a major or minor **chord**. DADF#AD is open D, DGDGBD open G and EGDGBE open E minor. There are many altered tunings like DADGAD which go beyond a simple **triad**. Open tunings are popular with folk fingerstyle players and for **bottleneck** playing, and have been used in a **rock** context by guitarists such as Jimmy Page of Led Zeppelin and Keith Richards of the Rolling Stones.

Opera
Large scale work for **orchestra** and singers, featuring narrative and characters, with defined song sections (**arias**) and recitatives (where a lyric is sung on one note). Operas can be tragic or comic, serious or light-hearted.

Opus
Literally meaning 'work', name used in classical music to catalogue a composition, e.g. Beethoven's Thirty-three Variations on a Waltz by Diabelli in C for piano, Opus 120.

Oratorio
C18th extended work for voices and an ensemble often with a sacred theme.

Orchestra
Largest ensemble of instruments with all types represented - strings, brass, woodwind, keyboard and percussion - regarded as the most powerful

combination in Western **classical** music.

Orchestration
The art of writing for an orchestra, or taking a piece first written for a solo instrument or small group and arranging it for an orchestra.

Ornaments
See **grace notes**.

Ostinato
(I) Lit. 'Persistent'. A musical figure constantly repeated, often in the **bass**.

Overtones
Higher parts of a note distinguished from the **fundamental**.

Overture
Piece of music originally intended as the introduction to a longer work but sometimes becoming popular enough to be played in its own right.

P

P. A.
Abbrev. for 'public address'. A sound system designed to amplify the voice or a small group of musicians. In a **rock** band microphones are usually placed in front of the **backline** amplifiers and then re-amplified by the P. A.

Pad
Recording term used to mean providing an unobtrusive chordal backdrop of some kind (often on a synth) behind the main lead instrument or voice.

Pan
To move a musical signal to the left or right of a stereo image during a mix. Late 1960s pop-rock records often used panning to give the music a pictorial quality, as can be heard on the **coda** of Jimi Hendrix's 'House Burning Down' (Electric Ladyland, 1968).

Parallel motion
Where musical parts move together in direction, as in Gregorian chant's consecutive **perfect fifths**.

Passing note
A note in the **harmony** which links two **chords**. Thus in the **bass** if moving from C major to A minor **chords** a B would link the two as a passing note.

Pedal point
A note repeated in the **bass** part while **chords** change and move above it. When this **bass** note is the key-note it is called a tonic pedal.

Pentatonic
A five note scale originally associated with oriental music. Much **lead guitar** soloing in **rock** and **blues** uses either the pentatonic minor (in A, A C D E G) or the pentatonic major (in A, A B C♯ E F♯).

Major, in A

minor, in A

Perfect cadence

A **chord** change from V to I at the end of a phrase, used to finish or establish a new key. The modulatory effect of a perfect cadence is strengthened if the V **chord** is turned into a **dominant** 7th.

	D	D7	G
	V	V7	I

Perfect Fifth

Interval of 3 1/2 tones naturally occurring between the 1st and 5th notes of a major or minor scale.

D Major   G Major

Perfect Fourth

Interval of 2 1/2 tones naturally occurring between the 1st and 4th note of a major or minor scale.

D Major   G Major

Phrasing

The art of grouping and interpreting notes in performance to give them expression.

Phrygian

One of the seven Greek **modes** or scales, the Phrygian **mode** is the **interval** sequence E F G A B C D E (the natural minor scale with a flattened 2nd).

E   F   G   A   B   C   D   E

Piano

(I) Volume direction meaning soft or softly.

Piano reduction

The condensing of music originally written for an ensemble onto a single piano part.

Pick-up

Device for electrically amplifying the sound of an **acoustic** instrument. See **humbucker**.

Pizzicato

Abbrev. pizz. Technique used by string players in which the string is plucked rather than bowed, creating a more percussive, but less sustained sound.

Plagal cadence

The **chord** movement IV to I at the end of a phrase.

	IV	I
	F	C

Plainsong
Type of sacred vocal music dating back a thousand years in Europe, sung in free **rhythm** from a four-line **stave**.

Plectrum
Also known as a pick, small piece of plastic used to strike the string of a guitar or mandolin. Plectra come in many shapes, sizes and thicknesses.

Pocket symphony
Informal term associated with American songwriter Brian Wilson, describing his increasingly ambitious vision, in the 1960s, of the pop song as a masterpiece of invention in miniature. Initially influenced by Phil Spector's wall of sound, this approach bore fruit on The Beach Boys' '*Pet Sounds*' and 'Good Vibrations' (1966).

Polyphony
Literally many voices, thus in music a piece in which there are interweaving melodies.

Portamento
(I) See **slur** and **glissando**.

Power-chord
(Colloq.) **Rock** term for a **perfect fifth**, with the root note and sometimes the fifth also doubled at a higher **octave**. Distorted fifths are crucial to the rhythm parts of heavier **rock** styles.

Pre-amp
Effects unit designed to boost the original signal.

Presto
(I) 'Quickly' (**tempo** indication).

Progressive rock
Once a term of approval but now often derogatory. Musical movement of the 1970s involving emphasis on virtuosity, increasing ambition and experimentation in the studio, a move away from the three minute 4/4 song, and lyrics that tried to go beyond pop's perennial boy-meets-girl themes. Attempts to mimic or borrow the forms of **classical** music (the creation of **rock** concertos and operas) revealed progressive rock's desire to satisfy the counter-culture's desire for its own 'high art'. Definitive prog-rock albums include *The Lamb Lies Down On Broadway* (Genesis, 1974), *Tales From Topographic Oceans* (Yes, 1974), and *Dark Side Of The Moon* (Pink Floyd, 1973).

Punk rock
Rock style characterised by brevity
(songs were rarely longer than a few
minutes), harmonic simplicity, fast
tempos, aggressive delivery and
sneering pitch-indifferent vocals. The
U.S. punk scene developed on the East
coast in the early 1970s; UK punk came
to prominence in late 1975-1977,
overthrowing the old progressive
musical order. Definitive punk rock
albums include *Never Mind The
Bollocks* (Sex Pistols, 1977), *London
Calling* (The Clash, 1979) and *The
Ramones* (The Ramones, 1976).

Q

Quadruple time
Another name for **common time**; four beats in a **bar**.

Quadruplet
Four notes played in the time it would normally take to play three of the same value. The quadruplet is to compound time what the triplet is to simple time.

Quantize
Technique of digital recording and electronic drum machines that automatically corrects slight deviances in timing thus producing a part that is perfectly in time.

Quartal harmony
A type of harmony where chord construction is based on the interval of a fourth rather than a third.

Quarter-tone
See **microtone**.

Quaver
Note which is an eighth of a beat, and half the length of a **crotchet**, or whole note. A **semiquaver** is half again, making it sixteenth of a beat.

Quintuple time
Five beats in a **bar**. The asymmetry of 5/4 is striking, especially in popular music. Dave Brubeck's '*Take Five*' (1960) is a typical example.

R

Raga

Indian music form involving scale-like figures which are taken as the basis for improvisation. Ragas have established associations in terms of their mood or the time when they are suitable to be performed.

Ragtime

Type of popular music from the early C20th immortalised by the piano instrumentals of Scott Joplin and an allusion in T. S. Eliot's poem *The Waste Land* (1922). Ragtime is marked by an inventive, almost comic **syncopation**. It was eventually subsumed into early **jazz**.

Rallentando

(1) Direction to slow down gradually. *Abbrev.* rall.

Rap

Musical style originating in the Afro-American community popular in the late 1980s and 1990s. **Melody** is replaced by a highly rhythmic delivery of rhymed, colloquial lyrics over a basic beat, often sampled. Influential artists include Public Enemy, Beastie Boys and De La Soul.

Rasguedo

Picking-hand technique used by **flamenco** guitarists involving explosive sequential uncurling of the fingers to strike the strings.

Real time

A term coined in the wake of the digital music revolution, to describe a non-programmed musical performance recorded at the same time as its intended duration.

Recapitulation

Generally, to re-state an earlier musical theme. More precisely this covers the third part of **sonata** form where the initial thematic material returns in the tonic key.

Recitative

Device used in an opera to communicate a lyric passage which is not suited to being harmonised in an elaborate manner. The words attempt to approximate the rhythms of speech and are chanted on one note.

Refrain

A repeated passage in a song equivalent to a **chorus**. In folk-song a line or lines that comes at the end of each verse.

Reggae

Jamaican popular music which developed in the 1960s and gained an international audience through the success of Bob Marley and The Wailers in the 1970s. Reggae is typified by electric instrumentation, simple harmonic changes (I-II is a favourite) and above all by its constant emphasis of the off-beat and short phrases on the electric bass which have distinct pauses between them. Other variants include Dub, where a piece is lengthened and subjected to extensive re-mixing including the foregrounding of the bass and the abrupt insertion of multi-tap echo. Lyrically, some reggae has strong links with Rastafarianism.

Related keys
See **Modulation**.

Relative key
Major and minor keys which share the same key-signature, but with one accidental raising the 7th degree of the minor scale. The relative minor is **chord VI** of the major key and is always a minor 3rd (three semitones) below the major key note. Eg:

G major	relative minor	E minor
F#	key signature	F# + D#

Resolution
General term for the release of a tension in music caused by a **dissonance** of some kind changing to a **consonance**.

Rest
Symbol used to indicate a period of silence in a **bar**. There are individual symbols for each equivalent note. Adding a dot after a rest increases its length by ½.

Reverb
Short for reverberation, the natural **acoustic** property of a space, characterised by a number of factors such as the length of echo. Reverb is an essential effect in the recording process, added at the mixing stage to give 'life' to a recording. Different periods of popular music have favoured different types of reverb, the 1980s, for example, using large amounts of reverb on drums. The 1990s have tended to favour a less 'wet' sound.

Rhapsody
A medium-length instrumental piece of no set form often for piano with a romantic or fantastic character. In popular music Gershwin's 'Rhapsody In Blue' and Queen's 'Bohemian Rhapsody' offer two highly contrasted examples.

Rhythm

One of the three foundations of most Western music, along with **melody** and **harmony**. Rhythm comprises the **tempo** of music, the type of beat, the number of beats in a **bar**, and the rhythm patterns generated by different instruments and melodic lines.

Rhythm and Blues (R'n'B)

Post-war Afro-American popular music having some gospel elements but also arising from the electrification of rural **blues** in cities like Chicago. As its name suggests, R'n'B has an emphatic **rhythm** and a tough, earthy quality, and is more of an ensemble style. It influenced rock'n'roll in the 1950s and groups like The Beatles, The Rolling Stones and The Who incorporated something of its feel in their early music. R'n'B itself persisted as a musical category through the 1960s despite yielding some of its territory to the smoother genre of 'soul'. Now also used to describe some modern soul and dance music.

Riff

(Colloq.) A short musical phrase of about 2 bars, which is the focus of interest in a piece of music, with any vocal **melody** that may be present. Riffs are essential to **rock** music, where they are played on the guitar. Deep Purple's 'Smoke On The Water' (1972), Cream's 'Sunshine Of Your Love' (1967) and Dire Straits' 'Money For Nothing'

(1985) are all riff-driven songs.

Risoluto

(I) Played in a resolute or bold manner.

Ritenuto

(I) Lit. 'held back'. Indication to play slower. Not a gradual slowing of **tempo** as indicated by rallentando.

Rock

Popular music form developed from a mixture of country, **blues** and **rhythm'n'blues**, exemplified first in the 1950s by the rock'n'roll songs of Elvis Presley, Little Richard, Chuck Berry et al, in the 1960s by The Beatles, The Rolling Stones, The Who and many others. Rock has in common with pop a grounding in the three or four minute song, with extensive repetition, a relatively simple harmonic vocabulary, and a fierce marking of the 4/4 beat. It differs from pop in being more aggressive, and lyrically and musically more experimental and adventurous. Pop has always been indifferent to being judged ephemeral; rock has often aspired to be taken seriously by 'high' culture.

Rockabilly

Type of 1950s American popular music which is closely related to rock'n'roll but places a stronger emphasis on the country elements in it. This is reflected in the choice of instruments, such as acoustic guitars and double bass. The energy and good-time feel of rockabilly made it popular for dancing.

Romanticism

A term used correctly in contrast to **classical** to describe the main trend of European music in the period 1790-1900. Romanticism saw both the composer and the **virtuoso** performer elevated to almost god-like status. Romantic music is concerned first and foremost with evoking emotion, hence it is dramatic, lyrical, dreamy, turbulent, and pushed beyond the forms and tonal rules of the C18th in order to achieve these effects. The outcome was the undermining of traditional tonality by composers like Wagner and Debussy.

Rondo

Compositional form in which an initial section in the tonic key is followed by a contrasting section, then the first section, then a third section, in the pattern ABACAD etc.

Root position

Chord in which the root note is the lowest. See **inversion**.

Round

Music for several voices in which after the first voice has completed its melodic phrase, the second voice begins with the same phrase, followed by a third and fourth while the first and second voices take up their next phrases.

Rubato

Expressive device by which the performer ignores the strict time of a piece, introducing pronounced pauses. Often used when playing C19th romantic music such as Chopin's Nocturnes.

S

Sampling
Electronic device popularised in the mid-1980s enabling the copying of a few seconds of sound which can then be manipulated on a **MIDI** synth or computer **sequencer**.

Sarabande
Instrumental dance popular in the C16th, in its later form becoming the third movement of a **Suite**.

Scale
Linear arrangement of notes, usually spanning one **octave**, from which the sense of **key** and **harmony** can be derived. Main forms include **major**, **minor**, **whole tone**, and **mode**.

Scat singing
Singing technique involving the improvisation of a tune, as though the voice were an instrument. To facilitate this, nonsense syllables - often alliterative - are used. Scat singing is a recognised jazz technique.

Second
Distance between C-D (major second) or C-D♭ (minor second) or reference to the second note of the scale.

Major 2nd   minor 2nd

Semi-acoustic
Type of hollow-body electric guitar fitted with pick-ups but able to produce some acoustic sound. Semi-acoustics have traditionally been popular with jazz players, in contrast to rock players who favour the solid-body electric.

Semibreve
Whole note, lasting for four beats of a 4/4 bar. A breve lasted four **minim** beats of 4/2 but is very rare in modern music.

1 - 2 - 3 - 4   1 - 2 - 3 - 4

Semiquaver
See **quaver**.

Semitone
Half of a **tone**: there are 12 in an **octave**.

Sequencer
Type of computer software which allows a piece of music to be programmed, edited, recorded and played back automatically. Information goes to the computer, usually from a **MIDI**

keyboard, but can also be entered and changed via the computer keyboard. Sequencing is to music what word-processing is to writing. Sequencers are phrase-based, pattern-based or linear.

Serenade

C18th instrumental piece designed to be played in the later evening. Modern connotation is of a gentle, lilting, romantic piece.

Seventh

Can refer to the **leading note** of a scale, or a chord. There are three main types of seventh **chord**: the **dominant** seventh (C E G B♭), the major seventh (C E G B) and the minor seventh (C E♭ G B♭)

Major 7th   C7   Cmin7

Sharp

Accidental, indicating the raising of a note by a **semitone**.

Sight-reading

The ability to sing or play a piece of music printed in traditional **notation** without ever having seen it before. Many musical examinations require demonstration of some ability to sight-read.

Simple time

Type of **rhythm** where the beat is always divisible by an even number. See also **duple** and **compound** time.

Sitar

Stringed instrument central to Indian music developed over a number of centuries, attaining its modern form in the last century. The sitar has a long neck and a small bowl-like body. The strings are not pressed against a fretboard (as with a guitar) but held down behind frets which are metal hoops. These curved frets enable the pitch of any given note to be raised almost an **octave** by simply pulling the string downwards. A set of secondary strings provide **drone** effects. The sitar is played with a small piece of wire fitted on the end of the finger. Western awareness of the sitar is mostly due to The Beatles' recordings and the concerts of Ravi Shankar.

Skiffle

Originally a black music form of the 1930s, skiffle was revived in poverty-struck post-war Britain by white teenagers in the 1950s. Skiffle was an energetic, three or four **chord** song form, played on unamplified instruments like **acoustic** guitar, harmonica, tea-chest bass, etc. It arose in the brief musical lull between the end of 1950s rock'n'roll and the tidal wave of beat music inspired by The Beatles. Its most famous exponent in the U. K. was Lonnie Donegan.

Slapback

A type of echo devised in the 1950s and heard on many of the early Sun recordings of Elvis Presley. The echo is a single repeat coming shortly after the original note.

Slide

Guitar technique. A **slur** from one note to another where the first is struck but the second is created simply by the movement of the finger. Also see **bottleneck**.

Slur

Technique where a player moves from one note to another by a smooth ascent or descent of pitch.

Snare

Part of the standard drum kit, the snare has a metal or wooden circular frame with a taut skin stretched across the top, and a set of metal wires underneath which vibrate when the skin is struck. The snare is the loudest, easiest-heard part of the kit and in popular music is responsible for driving the beat.

Sonata

Structure used for the first movement of a symphony and **concertos**. The sonata form is characterised by a First Subject, a Bridge section which changes **key** to the **dominant**, the **key** of the next theme - the Second Subject. These in total form the **Exposition**. After a double bar-line the music moves to the Development and eventually the **Recapitulation** using the First and Second Subjects.

Song cycle

A form devised by Schubert in the C19th where a number of songs could be linked to make a larger work.

Soprano

The highest span for the female voice, roughly from **middle C** to the second G above it.

Soul music

The term now covers many different styles of predominantly commercial Afro-American music. It originated in the 1960s, when elements of R'n'B, **blues**, and gospel were combined with a pop sensibility. The resulting mix, typified by much of the output of black artists on the **Motown**, Atlantic and Stax labels, was highly danceable yet with a stronger sense of **melody** and song structure than later dance music of the 1970s, 80s and 90s. Soul music is characterised by syncopated rhythms, a **harmony** that makes frequent use of minor 7 / major 7 **chords**, and a declamatory vocal style full of passion. Soul singers make extensive use of **melisma** in the 1990s with a rapid diminishing of emotional returns.

Soundcheck

Run-through before a live concert to test equipment is functioning and to enable the sound engineers to get a good mix.

Staccato
Type of note (with a dot above or underneath it) in which the duration of the note is curtailed.

Standard tuning
Guitar term for the usual tuning of E A D G B E in contrast to altered or **open tuning.**

Stave
Arrangement of five lines on which music is traditionally written. The type of **clef** used will determine which pitches a given stave covers.

Stepwise
A type of musical progression by **tone** or **semitone** increments.

Strat
Shortened form of Stratocaster, Leo Fender's world-famous 1950s electric guitar design. The Strat is characterised by three single-coil pickups, a five-way selector switch and a tremolo arm. The so-called 'superstrat' of the 1980s was an attempt by other companies to update the Strat design.

String Quartet
Ensemble consisting of four stringed instruments - first and second violin, viola and cello.

Subdominant
The fourth note and **chord** of the scale.

Subdominant (F)
Chord of F

Submediant
The sixth note and **chord** of the scale.

Submediant (A)
Chord of Am

Suite
A group of dances, originally in the classical suite in a single **key** and constructed in **binary form**. Although a range of dances could be featured, the staple forms were the **Allemande**, Courante, Gigue, **Minuet** and **Sarabande**.

Supertonic
The second note and **chord** of the scale.

Supertonic (D)
Chord of Dm

Suspension
Harmonic effect where tension is created and then resolved. The most common type is the suspended fourth and suspended second **chords**. In the first, C F G becomes C E G; in the second, C D G becomes C E G. On both instances the **third** is suspended, thus

rendering the chord neither major nor minor.

Sus4   Sus2

Swing feel
Rhythmic approach used in **blues** and **jazz** where the quarter-notes of simple 4/4 are played more as if they were the dotted quarter-notes of compound 12/8.

Sympathetic resonance
The ability of a string on an instrument to generate tones from other strings on the same instrument by vibrations travelling through its body. This is an important part of the colouration of the tone. Thus when the top E string on the guitar is played, part of the sound then heard depends on the bottom E (two octaves lower) vibrating 'in sympathy'.

Symphony
A large-scale work in four movements for **orchestra**.

Syncopation
Rhythmic effect created by holding notes over the beat and playing on the off-beat.

Synthesizer
Electronic keyboard developed in the 1960s capable of generating different sounds and wave-forms. The earliest were monophonic - only able to produce a single note at a time - but polyphonic synths soon became the norm. Digital sound greatly improved the authenticity of the synth's imitations of orchestral instruments.

Tabla

Small Indian hand-drum, tuned to different pitches, somewhat similar to bongos but with their own distinctive sound. Used to accompany the **sitar**.

Tablature

Alternate method of writing down guitar music where six lines represent the six strings and the fret-number of each note is written on the appropriate line. Early tablature such as that used for the lute in Elizabethan England also gave rhythmic indications.

Open strings of the guitar:

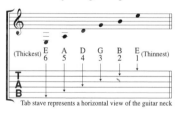

Tab stave represents a horizontal view of the guitar neck

Example of notation and TAB

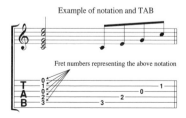

Fret numbers representing the above notation

Tapping

Technique popularised by U.S. electric guitarist Eddie Van Halen in the late 1970s, endemic in 1980s heavy rock, further developed by Steve Vai and Joe Satriani. The fretboard is struck with the fingers of the picking hand, generating fast **arpeggio** figures.

Techno

Type of popular music of the 1990s largely composed in the digital domain with **sequencers**, computers, samplers and drum machines, characterised by rapid **tempos**, an extremely simple **harmony**, sound effects, and an ethos which makes a virtue of the 'mechanical' impression such equipment easily produces.

Temperament

Most modern instruments use a system of tuning called '**equal temperament**' in which the **octave** is divided into twelve equal semitones all of which are slightly out of tune. Earlier systems included 'just' temperament which by making the **third** and fifth perfect created **chords** I, IV and V which were in tune.

Tempo

The speed of a piece of music. E.g:
[♩] = 120 b.p.m.

Tenor

Male voice part spanning from D in the centre of the bass clef to the first G on the treble **stave**.

Tenuto

(I) Lit. 'held'. Opposite to **staccato**, notes are held for their full length and sometimes even slightly extended.

Ternary

As **binary** consists of two sections, ternary consists of three: a first musical idea (section A) succeeded by a section B, and then section A repeated.

Tetrachord

Four notes separated by a tone, a tone, a tone and a semitone (C D E F). The **major scale** consists of two tetrachords.

Theremin

Electronic device devised in the 1930s which looks like a radio aerial and creates a field around it sensitive to movement. The player moves a hand within this field and the Theremin translates this into pitch. Used by The Beach Boys on 'Good Vibrations' (1966), various early 1960s TV themes, in concert by Jimmy Page of Led Zeppelin in the 1970s, and has enjoyed a revival of interest in the 1990s.

Third

Interval of either a major third (C-E, two tones) or a minor third (C-E♭, 1 1/2 tones). Also the third note of the **scale** and the middle note of a simple **triad** (C E G, C E♭ G).

Major 3rd   minor 3rd

Threshold

The level at which a sound processing effect switches on. A control marked 'threshold' is often seen on studio equipment such as compressors, noise gates and enhancers.

Tie

Line connecting two notes adding the duration of the second to the first. Only the first is played. Different to a **rest** in that it can continue across a bar-line.

Tierce de Picardie

(F) **Cadence** at the end of a minor **key** piece which causes the music to end in the minor's tonic major. Such a **cadence** in G minor would end on G major.

Timbre

The tonal quality of a voice or instrument.

Time code

Form of digital data used in recording which can be used to lock other instruments to play along with what has already been recorded.

Time signature

Two numbers at the beginning of a piece of music indicating the number of beats in a bar and the type of beat.

Toccata

(Lit.) 'Touch-piece'. A C17th piece for keyboard, exhibiting florid **scale** work and **broken chord** accompaniment. Often linked with the **fugue**.

Tone

(i) Distance between any two consecutive notes, typified by any two adjacent **white notes** except for E-F and B-C.

(ii) **Timbre** of an instrument or voice.

Tone poem

Also known as a symphonic poem, this is a one movement piece for **orchestra** intended to be in some way descriptive or narrative.

Tonic chord

Chord I of a **key**.

Tonic minor

Minor **key** which shares the same keynote as a major **key**. C minor is thus the tonic minor of C major (in contrast to the relative minor).

Transposition

The shifting of a piece of music from one **key** to another, sometimes to fit a vocalist's range. Also used as a compositional device, whereby a music phrase is repeated through different **keys**.

Transposing instruments

These instruments have their music written at a different pitch than the sound that they produce. Transposing instruments include all the brass instruments and most of the woodwind. The E♭ saxophone, for example, sounds a major 6th lower than written.

E♭ alto saxophone sounds a major sixth below the written pitch. Rule: **Written C sounds E♭**

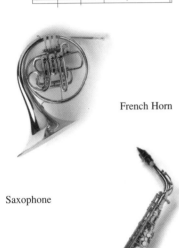

French Horn

Saxophone

Tremolando
(1) A technique involving the rapid re-striking of a note for its duration, rather than hitting the note once. Often used in string writing when the music requires a sense of drama and tension.

Tremolo
Sound effect for electric instruments which involves rapidly cutting off and then releasing the signal. It gives the notes a jagged, oscillating quality.

Tremolo arm
Device on an electric guitar attached to the tail-piece, allowing the strings to become movable and the player to slacken or raise the string-tension. Mild use creates the gentle **vibrato** heard on early 1960s recordings by The Shadows, more violent use creates spectacular glissandos, as can be heard vividly in Jimi Hendrix's performance of 'The Star-Spangled Banner' at Woodstock in August 1969.

Triad
A three note **chord**, for example, degrees 1, 3, and 5 of the **scale**.

Trio
In jazz, a popular three-musician ensemble, usually comprising drums, piano and double bass. In rock, the 'power-trio' comprises drums, electric bass and electric guitar. The 'power' epithet has come to be applied because such rock trios tend to play at high volume levels to mask the absence of a

harmony instrument if the guitar is soloing.

Triplet
Three equal notes played in the time of two. Approximates the skipping **rhythm** of compound time when in a **simple time**.

Tritone
The **interval** of three tones (e.g. C-F♯) known as the 'forbidden' or 'devil's' **interval** of medieval church music. Its dark discordant tone is essential to much 1980s **heavy metal**.

Truss rod
Metal rod that runs through the neck of steel-strung guitars allowing adjustments that can correct warping and other similar distortions which may set in over time.

Twelve-bar blues
Common form for **blues** and blues-derived music such as rock'n'roll. **Chord** I occupies bars 1-4, **chord** IV bars 5-6, **chord** I bars 7-8, and the last four bars are V, IV, I, V. This is usually in a major **key** but minor **key blues** also use this structure. There are many slight variants, such as the 'quick-change' **blues** where bar 2 is **chord** IV.

Twelve-note music
Atonal system devised by Schoenberg in the early C20th, replacing keys and scales with a twelve note series which is then developed by the composer throughout a piece.

Twin-neck
Type of guitar, usually electric, which has two necks attached to the body. The most popular configuration is a six-string with a 12-string, typified by the Gibson ES1275D, associated with Jimmy Page of Led Zeppelin and John McLaughlin of the Mahavishnu Orchestra. Often dismissed as symbols of rock pretension, these instruments do in fact offer significant musical potentials. The player may in the space of a single song contrast 6 string with 12 string sounds, or use two different tunings. These instruments also offer some stunning possibilities with sympathetic resonance.

Up beat
The unstressed beat that comes just before the bar line (in contrast to the down beat, the first of the next bar).

Ukelele
Small, short-necked instrument, originally related to the four-string Hawaiian guitar, popularised in the 1930s by the ukelele-banjo songs of George Formby Jnr.

Una corda
Direction to a pianist to depress the left, soft pedal, causing the hammers to only strike one string per note instead of three. The direction is ended with 'tre corda'.

Unequal voices
Somewhat anachronistic term for a vocal piece using male and female, i.e. mixed voices.

Unessential note
A note which is not part of the essential harmony, but is instead a passing or grace note.

Unison
Two notes of the same pitch.

Unison bend
Electric guitar technique for thickening phrases in **lead guitar** solos where two notes of the same pitch are generated. One is fretted, the other - usually a tone lower on the next string down - is bent to the required pitch.

Valve amp

Type of amplifier for electric instruments such as the guitar, utilising mid C20th vacuum-tube technology. The classic distortion of the rock guitar arose through guitarists over-stressing the valves in their amplifiers by playing at the highest volume the amp would permit. Valve amps are defined in contrast to solid-state transistor amps and, in the 1990s, digital amps.

Vamp

Verb and noun describing a simple chordal accompaniment to a song, originally consisting of triads in the left hand of a piano part, often extemporised from a chord sheet.

Variation

Compositional framework in which a theme is stated and then re-stated with shifting harmony and arrangement. Elgar's Enigma Variations is a famous example.

Verse

Important part of popular songs, along with Chorus and Middle Eight. If the verse lays out the lyrical problem or situation, the Chorus supplies an answer or a response.

Vibrato

Technique whereby a note is given expression by the movement of a finger as it holds down a string. This movement produces a subtle fluctuation in pitch. **Classical** vibrato moves up and down; rock guitar vibrato moves from side-to-side.

Viol

Early bowed string instrument popular in the C16th and C17th, ancestor of the modern violin family.

Violin

Small-bodied bowed instrument central to the orchestra, chiefly with a melodic function, tuned in fifths: G D A E.

Viola

Slightly deeper-toned version of the violin, tuned a fifth lower: C G D A. The orchestra's string section comprises viola with violin, cello and double bass.

Virtuoso

Anyone who has achieved a high degree of technical proficiency on an instrument.

Voicing

The choice of notes for a given chord. A simple triad has three notes but these could be played in many different pitches. These possibilities are each known as a voicing.

W

Wah-Wah
Foot-operated effect pedal which is connected in between the guitar and amplifier, altering the tone of a note to give a distinctly vocal effect. See Isaac Hayes' 'Theme From Shaft' (1971), the work of Melvin 'Wah-wah Watson' Ragin on many 60's Motown recordings, and Jimi Hendrix's intro to 'Voodoo Chile (Slight Return)' (1968) for some of the most famous uses of this gadget.

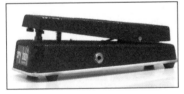

Walking bass
Bass style found in jazz and some rock'n'roll, which involves smooth, scale-like movement in eighth or quarter-notes.

Wall of sound
Phrase associated with 1960s record producer Phil Spector. It describes his approach to arranging pop songs, which involved filling the studio with an enormous number of musicians, thus greatly increasing the number of parts, the frequency range and the various

colours in the final mix.
Waltz
Popular C19th dance form in 3/4 time.

West Coast jazz
Style of restrained, improvisational jazz played by small ensemble, associated with California in the 1950s, and with performers such as Chet Baker and Dave Brubeck.

West Coast rock
Term describing a style of rock music played by US groups associated with California, San Francisco, etc. Its heyday ran from about 1966-75. It often features harmony vocals and a free-spirited, breezy, open feel. Influential groups might include The Byrds, Jefferson Airplane, Love, The Grateful Dead, Spirit, mid-70s Fleetwood Mac and The Eagles.

Wet
Adjective to describe the percentage of a signal which has been altered by a sound effect such as **reverb**, in contrast to the 'dry' unaltered signal. During the mixing process decisions are made about the blending of wet and **dry** signal.

White noise
Sound comprised of random electrically-generated frequencies fused together into a 'fuzzy' static.

White note
On the piano the white notes are C D E F G A B (in contrast to the black keys which are **sharps** and **flats**).

Whole-tone scale

A **scale** consisting of six notes extending over an **octave**. For example, starting on C: C D E F♯ G♯ A♯ C.

-tone-tone-tone-tone-tone-tone-

Wolf note

A note on the guitar rendered weaker than it should be by the **acoustic** idiosyncrasies of that particular instrument.

Word painting

Composition technique in Elizabethan madrigals where the movement or behaviour of a vocal line enacts the sense of the words. The word 'ascend' would have a rising melody; the word 'descend' a falling melody.

Xylophone

Percussion instrument consisting of bars of wood of different lengths to give different pitches, the top surface of each being slightly rounded. These are laid on a wooden frame and struck with small wooden hammers with rounded heads, creating a distinctive tonal but percussive sound.

Yodel

Singing technique associated with Alpine folk-song which involves extremely rapid fluctuations between a normal voice and falsetto.

Zither

A stringed instrument of the psaltery group, normally tuned A A D G C or A D G G C, designed to provide a single line melody with chordal accompaniment.

Further Reading

Check out some of the other books in this new series, listed below. These, and many other great titles, are available from all good music shops and book shops. Alternatively you can order from the Music Sales catalogue, or click on our website: **musicsales.co.uk.**

The Little Book of Tips and Tricks (for Guitar)
AM954767

This book has everything you need to know to improve your guitar technique, instantly! Sections on equipment, playing rhythm, how to solo, and how to play like the pros!

The Little Book of Love Lyrics
AM954822

The lyrics to 35 of your favourite old and new love-songs, including 'Could It Be Magic', 'I Will Always Love You', 'Take My Breath Away' and 'Wonderful Tonight'.

The Little Book of Chords (for Guitar)
AM954778

A bite-size chord book with fully-illustrated chord diagrams and photos for hundreds of useful chords, including triads, major and minor chords, slash chords, power-chords, sevenths/ninths, sus chords and many more!

The Little Book of Music Theory
AM954855

An introduction to Music Theory, including sections on accidentals, rhythm, major and minor keys, intervals, modes and chords. The perfect accompaniment to The Little Book of Musical Terms!

Music Sales Limited Newmarket Road Bury St Edmunds Suffolk IP33 3YB
Tel: 01284 702 600